Remembering our past, we think naturally
of the future. No institution is more concerned
with the future than a university.

WILLIAM E. LAVERY, *1976*

Grateful acknowledgment is hereby given for permission to reprint excerpts from *The First 100 Years: A History of Virginia Polytechnic Institute and State University,* by Duncan Lyle Kinnear. Copyright © 1972 by Virginia Polytechnic Institute Educational Foundation, Inc. Reprinted by permission of the publisher.

Special thanks to Charles M. Forbes, William T. Walker, Jr., F. Duke Perry, and the Virginia Tech Foundation, Inc.

The photographs of this book are dedicated to the Mellott family and to Robert Llewellyn.

Designed by Josef Beery and Jim Gibson. Edited by Ross A. Howell, Jr.

Library of Congress Catalog Card Number: 86-81076

ISBN 0-9616878-0-0

Printed and bound in Hong Kong by Everbest Printing Co., Ltd. for Four Colour Imports, Ltd., Louisville, Kentucky.

Published by Howell Press, Inc., 2000 Holiday Drive, Charlottesville, Virginia 22901. Telephone (804) 977-4006.

HOWELL PRESS

VIRGINIA TECH
A PORTRAIT

INTRODUCTION BY G. BURKE JOHNSTON   PHOTOGRAPHY BY JACK MELLOTT

Preface

THERE ARE EVENINGS AT VIRGINIA TECH WHEN ONE CAN walk out on the Drill Field by the pylons of Memorial Chapel and sense the full breadth of the campus. The lights of modern academic buildings and dormitories reach from horizon to horizon, quite a different vista from the cluster of buildings that once made up the campus.

The university has experienced remarkable change. In the last two decades alone, enrollment has grown from 7,000 students to more than 22,000. Sixty-eight degree programs and two academic colleges have been added to the curriculum. Annual expenditures for research have increased twelve-fold to $60 million. The university's public service programs now reach throughout the Commonwealth of Virginia and even overseas.

These developments seem far removed from the small, land-grant college founded here in 1872.

Yet on those evenings, in the stillness, one can also sense the tradition and permanence of the university. Over the last century, generations have savored the rich colors of a mountain autumn, or worked late into the night on a difficult class assignment, or huddled against the wind on a February morning, or moved to the rhythm of a favorite song at a dance. Perhaps they even stood some evening at this same place, thinking of the past and future.

That shared experience is the essence and pride of Virginia Tech. Each generation has affirmed its commitment to service and excellence. The remarkable changes that have occurred here are in fact expressions of principles that have guided the institution for over a century—accessible educational opportunity, rigorous research and application in diverse fields of learning, and a tradition of extending knowledge to improve the lives of all citizens.

The pages that follow suggest the essence and vitality of Virginia Tech. G. Burke Johnston brings a unique perspective to these images. His service as teacher, scholar, and dean spans the dramatic, half-century "metamorphosis" of the university. Jack Mellott, a talented young artist, worked from dawn to dusk and between his class hours as a student to make the photographs for this book.

What emerges is a beautiful, lasting portrait of Virginia Tech.

W. E. Lavery

WILLIAM E. LAVERY
President

9

Metamorphosis MY FIRST ACQUAINTANCE WITH VIRGINIA

Polytechnic Institute began in the spring of 1930. The stock market crash had taken place the fall before, and the Great Depression had started. Graduate students (not for the first or the last time) were worried about finding teaching jobs. When Dr. Carol Montgomery Newman, head of the English department at VPI, wrote to me at Columbia University that spring, offering an instructorship in English beginning in September, I accepted with enthusiasm.

In those days, when automobiles were far from numerous, much travel was by rail. Passengers for Blacksburg got off the train at the Christiansburg station of the Norfolk and Western Railway. There was a little spur line from Christiansburg to Blacksburg; the train nicknamed the "Huckleberry," but passengers usually teamed up and took a taxi, letting the "Huckleberry" bring trunks and other baggage to the Blacksburg station. (Trunks now seem almost as obsolete as passenger trains.)

Blacksburg offered a magnificent setting in the Virginia mountains, and the fall of 1930 was a gorgeous one.

All the faculty, all the students, and all the townspeople were strangers to me. The University Club on the VPI campus had been built fairly recently; many bachelor faculty members, young and not-so-young, roomed and boarded there. Seated at tables for four in the dining room, we were served three meals a day. My table was made up of assistant professors and instructors in English, and founded for me three long friendships.

Dr. Newman turned out to be an admirable employer. He was a very active man who had served for a time as dean of the academic department as well as professor and head of the English department. During World War I he was secretary of the YMCA. He was secretary of the athletic council for about a quarter of a century. Among his many activities was bringing to the community plays and movies for entertainment and cultural benefits. He was noted as a lecturer both on and off campus. Perhaps his most popular lecture was "American Humor," especially appropriate for his twinkling eyes and his delight in sharing laughter. In those days many of the faculty bore nicknames. Dr. Newman, because of his small size and quick movements, was called "Froggy."

Dr. Newman and his wife, "Miss Carrie," made the department of English and foreign languages more like a family than an academic organization. The Newmans gave me my introduction to the campus itself. They lived on "Faculty Row," which extended through the campus and was a vital part of the college community. The Row and the campus furnished material for an interesting portrait gallery.

The President of the College, Dr. Julian Ashby Burruss, was one of the old-style Roman-emperor college presidents. He was a man of very firm opinions. One principle he insisted upon was that no class should have more than 30 students in it. To most of the faculty, especially the younger ones like me, he seemed austere and remote if not down-right formidable. At his first faculty meeting he informed us that we might not see him again that year. Few of us did, except at his formal reception at the President's mansion. He reached faculty and students chiefly through John Edward Williams, dean of the college, and Paul Neyron Derring, YMCA secretary. (Dr. Duncan Lyle Kinnear, in his book *The First 100 Years: A History of Virginia Polytechnic Institute and State University*, made it clear that Dr. Burruss was much more warm and human than his forbidding facade indicated.)

In those days of comparatively small enrollments and a small faculty, several faculty members had to wear more than one hat. John E. Williams, for example, in addition to serving as dean of the college, was professor and head of the department of mathematics, vice-president without portfolio, and director of admissions without title. These academic functions were supplemented by his position as member of the athletic council. Dean Williams was a diplomat with political talent. His friendly relations covered students and staff and stretched across the state of Virginia. It was said that if an enraged person entered his office, the dean, calm and unruffled, would take time to light his pipe, very deliberately, and then "smoke at" the indignant one until he was completely calmed.

Paul N. Derring, YMCA secretary, had been blinded in his boyhood in a serious accident, but had pushed on with great fortitude in his education and career, being elected to Phi Beta Kappa at the College of William and Mary and dedicating himself to religious work through the YMCA. He had phenomenal ability to recognize and remember voices and could call a name after not "seeing" a friend or acquaintance for years (and he always used the word "seeing"). His handicap and his heroic rising above it no doubt helped him to reach students, even those difficult to reach. Dr. Burruss used Derring's gifts wisely. Paul Derring was probably the most beloved figure on the campus during the first century of the school.

The most prominent name in VPI athletics in the first century of the school was beyond doubt Clarence P. "Sally" Miles. (I never did learn how this rugged football and baseball player came by his amazing nickname.) Like Dean Williams, he wore many hats, perhaps more than any other staff member. By the end of what may be called the first act of my experience here, he had already been professor of foreign languages, coach of football, graduate chairman of athletics, and athletic director. The college's first stadium, where both football and baseball were played, was completed in 1926 and named in his honor. (Miles was, of course, in Tuscaloosa in 1932 when VPI came very close to winning the football championship of the Southern Conference, which then was composed of teams now in the Southeastern Conference, the Southern Conference, and the Atlantic Coast Conference. Not many people now remember that in 1932 with victories over Roanoke College, Georgia, Maryland, William and Mary, Kentucky, and Washington and Lee under its belt, VPI played the University of Alabama and almost spoiled its Homecoming. VPI scored first and led six to nothing at half time. Late in the third quarter Alabama scored a safety, then a touchdown and extra point, and won the game nine to six. After that major disappointment, the team defeated the University of Virginia and VMI to post one of its best records.)

The most Olympian dweller on Faculty Row was William Henry Rasche, professor of mechanism and descriptive geometry. A leonine man whose "good morning" had the hint of a roar as well as a salutation, Professor Rasche looked like an amplified William Shakespeare and bore the nickname "Bosco." (Some student had been to a carnival exhibiting a wild man called Bosco and brought back the name for the formidable professor.) Once a green freshman called Professor Rasche "Professor Bosco" in class. The report was that the First Academic Building, where the class was being held, shook on its foundations.

In the 1930s the most striking thing to a visitor on campus was certainly the Corps of Cadets. Students in the Corps wore their uniforms to class, on the campus, to church, and in the town of Blacksburg. On the Upper Quadrangle in the afternoons, sufferers could be seen "walking tours" to remove demerits. They wore dark blue formal blouses with white cross-belts and white gloves and walked with rigidly erect bodies and military stride. There were of course many parades, in which the excellent military band, the Highty-Tighties, played a prominent part. On Thanksgiving Day the major athletic event of the year took place in Roanoke: the VPI-VMI football game. The VPI Corps was transported on the "Huckleberry" to Roanoke. Both the VPI Corps and the VMI Corps marched from downtown Roanoke to Victory Stadium. I doubt that a major bowl game now could match the intensity of that annual event in the old days.

The Corps was involved with most of the social activity on campus during this era. Women students had been admitted since 1921, but their number was small, and male civilian students were far from numerous. The German Club and the Cotillion Club sponsored several formal dances each year. Of course, they were not attended exclusively by cadets and their dates, but formal uniforms were very prominent. During my years on the faculty in the early '30s there was no ring dance. The first one did not take place until the spring of 1934, just after I left.

By the spring of 1933 the Great Depression was tightening its hold; all state salaries were cut, finally by 20 percent across the board. Since that left me with little chance to save more money for graduate study, I went back to Columbia University to work on a doctorate. Seventeen years elapsed before I rejoined the VPI faculty in 1950.

The winds of change — nay, the hurricanes of change — had been blowing. In classical mythology people were sometimes changed to stone, trees, rivers, stars, or constellations to memorialize the significance of their lives. The most notable collection of stories about these changes is Ovid's *Metamorphoses*. I would like to take a leaf from Ovid and discuss two kinds of metamorphosis that have occurred at VPI.

The first of these is the dramatic change of the institution itself from a small agricultural and mechanical school to the large complex multiversity it is today. This metamorphosis began as far back as Dr. John McLaren McBryde's administration in the 1890s and has gathered momentum through the years.

World War II was no doubt responsible for the greatest change. The onrush of veterans back to college affected all the institutions of higher learning in the country, but the predominantly military schools were most drastically affected. Seasoned veterans of the war had no intention of signing up for more military service. At VPI two student governments, in effect two student bodies, sprang up, and the power and prestige of the Cadet Corps diminished. Years later the military requirement was dropped altogether. While the Corps has been much reduced in number, it is still a vital part of the tradition of the institution.

There were major academic changes following my return to VPI in 1950. Mathematics, which had been only a service department when I first taught here, offered both undergraduate and graduate degrees. Business administration became a school; the department of history and political science was formed and placed in the new school of science and general studies.

Changes that had begun in the 1950s were much accelerated in the 1960s and '70s under the leadership of Presidents T. Marshall Hahn, Jr. and William E. Lavery. Hitherto undreamed-of metamorphoses occurred. The liberal arts departments ceased to teach only service courses and became degree-granting departments. Following the recommendation of the Virginia Higher Education Study Commission, the state legislature recognized that the institution was in fact a university, and allowed the word "university" to be included in the title; the "schools" became "colleges." Virginia Polytechnic Institute and State University, more popularly known as Virginia Tech, grew to seven colleges and a graduate school. The most recent addition to the university's academic programs, the college of veterinary medicine, brings the total number of colleges to eight.

The tremendous growth of the school has of course greatly expanded the physical plant. A second type of metamorphosis, the figurative changing of men and women into stone, brick, and glass, is an important part of that growth.

When I returned to VPI in 1950, the grand landscape was the same, but the campus was very different. The most notable physical difference was the addition of Burruss Hall, which, as "Miss Carrie" Newman said, "split Faculty Row like the Great Wall of China." During the 1950s and '60s, the march of majestic stone buildings wiped out Faculty Row. The First Academic Building, which had withstood the shock of the freshman calling Professor Rasche "Professor Bosco," was destroyed and replaced by Rasche Hall, a dormitory. The Second Academic Building, home of the department of English and foreign languages, was also replaced by a dormitory.

"Sally" Miles must be the holder of the most remarkable number of metamorphoses in the history of the institution. Keeping his athletic connection as faculty chairman of athletics, he succeeded John Williams as dean of the college (the last) and returned to teaching as professor of German. Miles Stadium, dear to his heart, had to be sacrificed to make space for more student housing. Miles Hall, a dormitory, and an endowed professorship in his name in the college of arts and sciences preserve his memory.

Two faculty members honored with buildings reached their tenth decade: Frank L. Robeson and Claudius Lee.

Frank Robeson joined the faculty in 1904 and retired in 1954. He was the author of a successful physics textbook for college freshmen and was a masterful teacher. Even in his long retirement his former colleagues sent him apparently hopeless cases to salvage if possible; many were salvaged. He said his policy was to charge a tutorial fee if the student drove up to his house in a car better than his—no fee if the car was worse than his. He lived to attend the dedication of Robeson Hall, the present home of the physics department.

Claudius Lee and the Virginia Agricultural and Mechanical College were born the same year — 1872. Lee attended the convocation celebrating the centennial of the Morrill Land-Grant Act and the 90th anniversary of VPI. He took pride in the fact that as an undergraduate he had named *The Bugle*, the college annual. Professor of electrical engineering, he was a sympathetic and beloved teacher. Late in life, at a meeting of a student-faculty group, he said: "Since I have been here, everything has changed except two: I am the same, and you students are the same."

Many of the grand old faculty members of the past have undergone the metamorphosis of having their names placed in brick and stone. While it is the natural course of time, it is sad that today few students and few faculty members who cross the campus have any picture of the men and women whose names are memorialized in the buildings — Hutcheson Hall (for two brothers, Thomas B. and John R.), Walter S. Newman Hall, Carol M. Newman Library, Paul Derring Hall, John E. Williams Hall, Norris Hall, Whittemore Hall, Maude E. Wallace Hall, Clarice Slusher Hall, Cassell Coliseum, and more. Those of us who are old walk by those buildings and think of flesh and blood.

There is pleasure in seeing the new buildings named for many of those individuals I remember so well. They were people whose dedication to learning, whose commitment to service, and whose colorful personalities contributed to the special character of this place. Surely their spirits abide here, among the new faces and buildings, reaching generations of students who have never heard their voices, have never seen their faces.

Without being endowed with the gift of prophecy, I would venture to suggest, given my experience, that in the future there will be many more metamorphoses.

G. BURKE JOHNSTON
Blacksburg, Virginia
May 1986

My two boys left this morning
for your college. Charles is a husky boy
and will get along. William is in
poor health. Please see that he wears his hat
and coat when the weather is bad.

LETTER TO JOHN M. MCBRYDE, *ca. 1900*

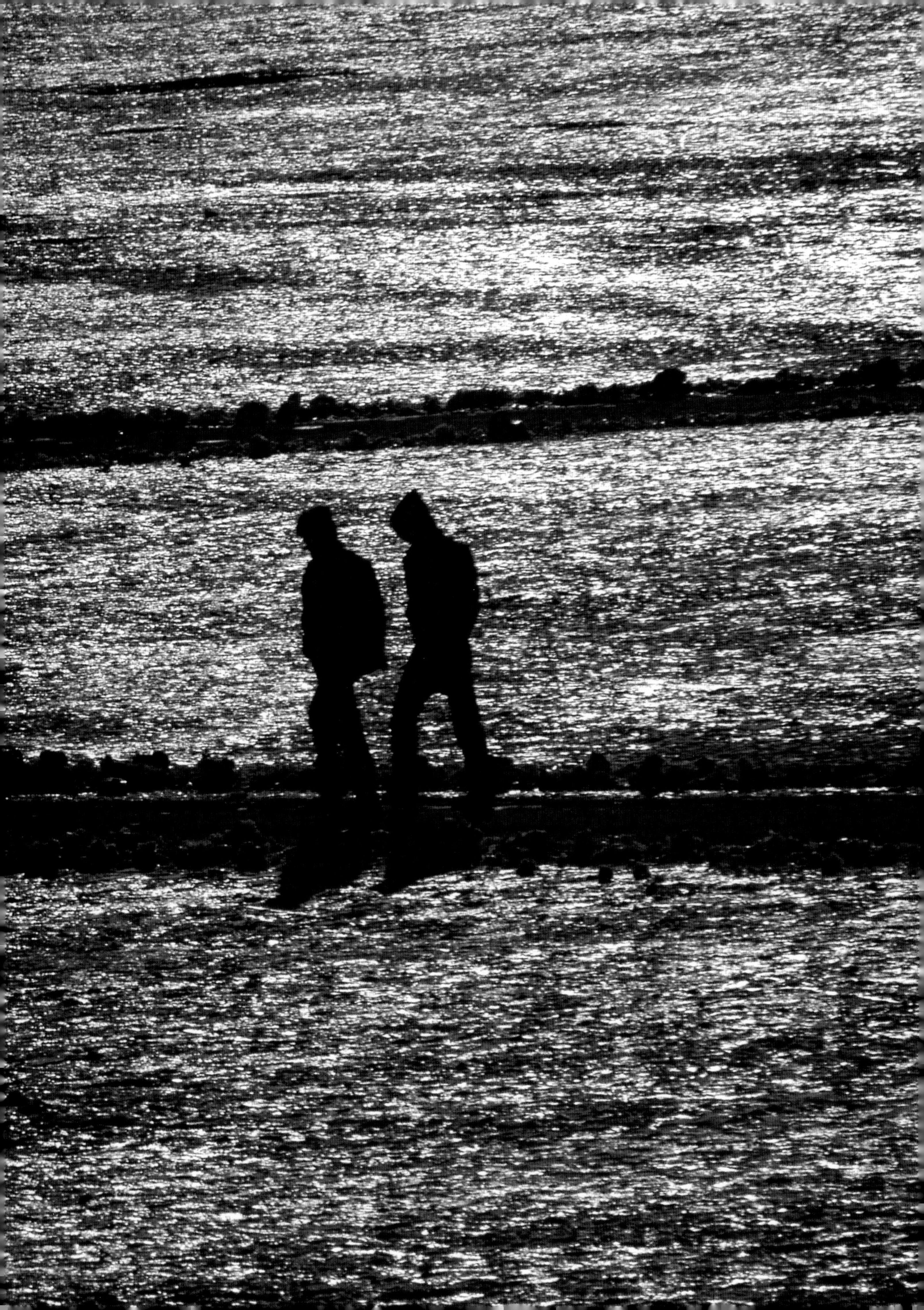

The college shall be so organized...as to teach all
the classical and scientific subjects, as well
as such as relate more immediately to agriculture and
mechanics...such a course of instruction
will promote liberal as well as practical education.

BOARD OF VISITORS, *1878*

$$\text{size} = \sqrt{\text{value for place}}$$

$$\sqrt{\text{value of bar}}$$

$$= \sqrt{10,000}$$

$$\sqrt{100}$$

or

There was no idea of team play; whoever got the ball — by luck — ran with it; no one knew anything about interference, and tho' we had a system of signals, it was a question of luck how each play went…the boundaries of the field were marked off with a plough, as also the 25-yard lines. The field was not as smooth as the bed of the new Blacksburg railroad, but ran up and down hill, with interesting little hollows which hid the play from spectators on the other side of the field.

FOOTBALL PLAYER, *1892*

Hoki, Hoki, Hoki Hy!
Tech! Tech! V.P.I.!
Sola-Rex Sola-Rah
Polytech-Vir-gin-i-a!!
Rae, Ri, V.P.I.

"OLD HOKIE" YELL, *ca. 1893*

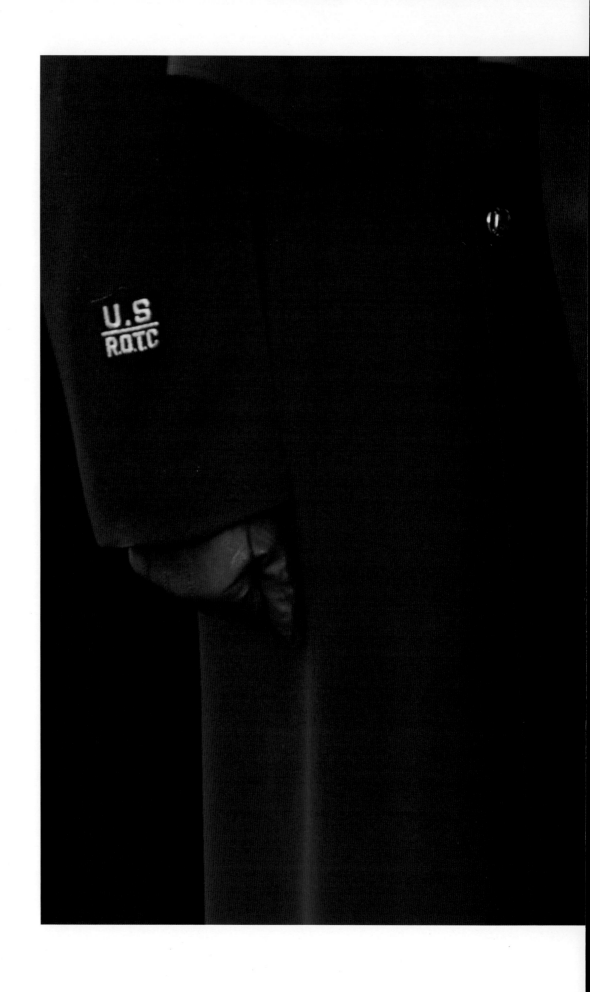

In a time of stress and danger, when
the government called
for men trained militarily, VPI said
at once, "We are ready."

JOSEPH D. EGGLESTON, JR., *1917*

The great stone pylons stand tall on the
memorial at Virginia Tech. On them are sculptured
larger than life stone figures, poised in
endless vigil, mute reminders of a proud heritage.
They stand, fittingly, above a chapel. Their
message is eternal. They speak of loyalty and honor,
brotherhood and duty, leadership and service.

T. MARSHALL HAHN, JR., *1967*

No doubt you get a lot of letters from fathers telling
you all about the fine qualities of their
sons. Well I love my son very dearly but so far as books
are concerned I have not discovered any fine
qualities yet. Will you take him in your school and see
if your professors can find any?

LETTER TO JOHN M. MCBRYDE, *ca.1900*

The University…insists upon one basic
principle — that no set of beliefs or interpretations may
impose rigid limits upon the inquiring mind.
The discovery of the unknown amidst the order and
beauty of physical reality, whether in a
microscopic cell or out among the stars, is its
highest calling.

WILLIAM E. LAVERY, *1979*

NOTES

1 VAWTER HALL   Charles E. Vawter, Rector of the Board of Visitors 1889-1900, played a vital role in implementing President John M. McBryde's expanded academic programs, which led ultimately to the modern university of today. Vawter Hall, named in his honor, has served as a student dormitory since 1962.

2-3 PRICE HALL   The distinctive stone for Virginia Tech's campus buildings is quarried in nearby Ellett Valley.

4-5 MEMORIAL CHAPEL PYLONS   Dedicated in 1960, Memorial Chapel features eight sculptured Indiana limestone pylons representing the ideals of Virginia Tech: Service, Loyalty, Duty, Ut Prosim ("That I May Serve," the university's motto), Brotherhood, Honor, Leadership, and Sacrifice. The names of alumni who have died in military service are carved on the pylons.

6 ALUMNI HALL   The dormers of Alumni Hall bring a Georgian architectural flavor to the predominantly Gothic architecture of the campus. The first meeting of the Alumni Association was held on August 11, 1875, when the 12 members of the first graduating class met and elected officers for their alumni organization.

8 BURRUSS HALL   The vaulted ceiling of the foyer is visible through the Gothic window above the main entrance to Burruss Hall.

10 UNIVERSITY CLUB   Organized by a faculty group in 1925, the University Club is a meeting place for faculty and townspeople. The club house was completed in 1930.

16 FIELD, PRITCHARD HALL   Many students refer to the open field in front of Pritchard Hall as "the Prairie." Pritchard is the largest dormitory on campus, housing 1,040 students.

17 DUCK POND   A faculty committee recommended the construction of a lake suitable for "boating and swimming in the summer and skating in the winter," but the plan was scaled down. The lake, or "Duck Pond," as it was nicknamed by students, was built in the summer of 1937.

18 DUCK POND

19 AERIAL VIEW, PRESIDENT'S HOME   Located in "the Grove," the building has housed university chief executives from the time John M. McBryde moved there in 1902 until T. Marshall Hahn, Jr. moved to a privately built home in 1971. There are plans to refurbish the structure so that it might be used again as the President's residence.

20-21 AERIAL VIEW   The university is situated on a plateau between the Blue Ridge and Allegheny Mountains some 2,100 feet above sea level. The ridge in the background of the photograph is the eastern continental divide.

22 SLUSHER HALL   Contrasting with this high-rise dormitory are Smyth Hall, a stone building, and Hillcrest Hall, a brick structure.

23 PRICE HALL   Completed in 1907, the building cost $20,900 to construct; it is named for Harvey L. Price, who served as dean of agriculture 1908-1945.

24 DRILL FIELD   Virginia Tech's eighth President, Julian A. Burruss, described a plan for the campus in 1924 that included a central "recreation and drill field" that was "to be left open forever." The Drill Field has served Virginia Tech students as a horticultural garden, military training ground, and intramural athletic site.

25 SEITZ HALL   Prominently positioned on the "Aggie Quad," the building was named for Charles E. Seitz, who retired as head of agricultural engineering in 1954. During the depression, agricultural engineering staff designed the structure; trained transient laborers in stonecutting, masonry, plumbing, carpentry, and electricity; and oversaw much of the construction.

26-27 DRILL FIELD   Called "the Monster" by generations of students who have crossed it during the winter, the Drill Field gained the nickname by virtue of the icy winds that blow from the Allegheny Mountains.

28 BURRUSS HALL   Burruss houses administrative and faculty offices and a 3,003-seat auditorium. The cornerstone was laid at the 1935 commencement, and one year later the first commencement was held inside the auditorium.

29 HILLCREST HALL   The first residence built specifically to house women students, Hillcrest has been known by several generations of Virginia Tech students as the "Skirt Barn."

30 WIND TUNNEL   The facility is capable of generating winds with a maximum velocity of 175 miles per hour.

31 CASCADE TUNNEL   This special wind tunnel is used to study the flow of air around compressor blades.

32 CLASSROOM, WILLIAMS HALL   More than 1,400 men and women make up Virginia Tech's faculty. Three professors comprised the college's first faculty in 1872: James H. Lane, professor of mathematics and foreign languages; Charles Martin, professor of English and ancient languages; and Gray Carroll, professor of mathematics.

33 CAROL M. NEWMAN LIBRARY   Named for an outstanding professor of English, the library contains over 1.5 million volumes. Its computerized cataloging system has served as a model for libraries throughout the country.

34 RESEARCH LABORATORY   Solid-state electronics is one of more than 3,000 topics being investigated by Virginia Tech researchers.

35 FOYER, BURRUSS HALL   The building was called the Teaching and Administration Building until 1944, when the Board of Visitors by unanimous vote changed the name to Julian A. Burruss Hall.

36-37 BURRUSS HALL

37 COLUMNS, BURRUSS HALL

38 BALLET PRACTICE, MEMORIAL GYMNASIUM   As a comprehensive university, Virginia Tech has broadened its curriculum to embrace the performing arts.

38-39 UNIVERSITY CHORUS AND ORCHESTRA   Both student and faculty musicians perform in the university's groups.

40 DRILL FIELD   The early warmth of spring draws students out of the library for continued study.

41 BURRUSS HALL   Additions in 1968 and 1970 have more than doubled the original size of Burruss Hall.

42 APPLE ORCHARD   Delicious apples growing in an experimental plot near campus are the product of the university's traditional commitment to agriculture, embodied in the Virginia Cooperative Extension Service and a series of agricultural experiment stations.

43 HOMECOMING PARADE   A young Hokie enjoys a high-level view of the annual event.

44 HIGHTY-TIGHTIES   Band company of the Corps of Cadets, the Highty-Tighties won first place in the 1953, 1957, and 1961 Presidential Inaugural Parade band competition, a feat never equaled by any other band and possibly one of the reasons the competition is no longer held.

45 TRUMPETER, HIGHTY-TIGHTIES   The first co-ed marching rank of the Highty-Tighties performed at football games during the 1971 season.

46-47 LANE STADIUM   Dedicated in 1975 with a 22-14 victory over the University of Virginia, the facility presently seats 52,000.

47 FOOTBALL PLAYERS   The first campus game of "Rugby football" was played on a field behind Barracks Number One, now Lane Hall, in the autumn of 1891.

48 ALUMNUS, HOMECOMING PARADE   Adopted in 1896, the university colors of Chicago maroon and burnt orange are familiar elements in the fall landscape at Virginia Tech.

48-49 ALUMNI BAND, HOMECOMING PARADE   The performance of alumni "Marching Virginians" is a rousing part of Homecoming festivities.

50-51 CASSELL COLISEUM   With 9,876 permanent seats, the coliseum hosts Metro Conference basketball action.

52 LANE HALL   Dominating the "Upper Quad," Lane Hall was completed in 1888. The structure is named for James H. Lane, first commandant of cadets.

53 NEWMAN HALL

54-55 CORPS OF CADETS   Generations of new Corps

members have been ironically told that U.S. ROTC is an acronym for "U Stay Right On This Campus," a reference to the strict off-campus visitation rules implemented in the 1890s. Some 700 men and women are presently enrolled in the voluntary organization. The dark blue overcoat with cape lined in red was introduced to Corps uniforms in 1920.

56 MEMORIAL CHAPEL PYLONS Sculptor Charles Rudy designed the pylons of the Memorial Chapel.

57 MEMORIAL CHAPEL PYLONS This evening view of the pylons brings to mind Fred Waring's "Moonlight and VPI," a song composed for the 1942 Ring Dance.

58 COLUMN, MEMORIAL GYMNASIUM In 1919, Virginia Tech alumni raised funds to erect the gymnasium, which commemorates graduates who lost their lives in World War I.

59 MEMORIAL CHAPEL

60-61 AERIAL VIEW The wilderness of Brush Mountain and Poverty Creek lies just west of campus.

62 AERIAL VIEW The small pond between the Duck Pond and the Drill Field is called the "Ice Pond." It supplied ice to the college until a refrigerating plant was opened in the 1898-1899 academic session.

63 DUCK POND

64 FLOWER BED, ALUMNI HALL Salvia and marigolds brighten the campus during summer months.

65 ALUMNI HALL Originally built in 1935, this columned structure has served as the Faculty Center and the Continuing Education Center.

66 COMMENCEMENT In 1881, William H. Ruffner commented on the service he believed land-grant institutions should provide. "These colleges," he wrote, "must work among the people, not above them. The people must understand the col-lege, and love it, and be proud of it." Each year commencement in Blacksburg witnesses that pride.

67 COMMENCEMENT Virginia Tech annually graduates more than 4,000 men and women, the largest commencement in the Commonwealth of Virginia.

68-69 AERIAL VIEW The rugged Allegheny Mountains rise to a height of more than 4,300 feet a few miles north of Blacksburg.

70 MCBRYDE HALL Named for the university's fifth President, John M. McBryde Hall is a general academic building. Sometimes called "the Father of Modern VPI," President McBryde oversaw the renovation of six buildings and the construction of 67 new buildings during his administration 1891-1907.

71 CAROL M. NEWMAN LIBRARY Sunrise outlines the curving profile of Newman Library and the cupola of Alumni Hall.

73 BURRUSS HALL The Burruss tower houses an electronic carillon installed in 1958.

74-75 ALUMNI HALL A student choir lights the university Christmas tree.

76 OFFICERS, CORPS OF CADETS The first cadet uniforms cost $17.25 and consisted of a cadet gray cap, jacket, and trousers trimmed with black.

78 BIOCHEMISTRY AND NUTRITION BUILDING

80 ACADEMIC MANTLE AND ROBES "Our most earnest desire," wrote Walter S. Newman, President of the university 1947-1962, "is to dedicate the complex facilities of this institution to furthering the advance of agriculture, business, and industry to preparing our youth proficiently in the vocations, and at the same time, to develop human beings informed with humility and, thereby aware of their social privileges and duties."